Made
in Ilkley

Growing up in a small town
in the 1940s and 1950s

Written and illustrated
by Diana Crawshaw

ISBN 978-0-9574415-4-5

Published in 2020 by
Caroline Brannigan, Richmond, North Yorkshire

This book is dedicated to my Grandpa, William Bradley, who always told me, "Anything is possible, if you put your mind to it!" With thanks to Roger Davy, for introducing me to my publisher, Caroline Brannigan and to my brother Ian Crawshaw, whose great patience and computer skills made this book's journey from dog-eared notebooks to publication possible. Special thanks to Peter Atkins, Sheila Edwardes and Chris Horner for their vital backing and support.

Bonfire Night

In the sad autumn mist, the giant horse chestnut trees let their golden-fingered leaves drop onto the black road that tumbled under the railway arch to the river beyond. It was the time of conkers at last, with the shiny red jewels emerging from prickly green cases, briefly new and gloriously perfect at the beginning, then growing duller after a few days in your blazer pocket. One day the drawer in the bedroom jammed stubbornly after being filled with conkers for safekeeping by my brother.

It was also the time for chumping. Any fallen branch and some, not quite fallen, but persuaded to give up by one or two boys suspended on the conveniently low-hanging parts, fell with a loud crack onto the road below.

As more branches were gathered, the scene was like one of medieval peasants harnessed with ropes to the increasingly unwieldy cargo and hauling merrily, chattering and coughing in the foggy autumn air. Cars had to reposition themselves smartly on narrow roads, seeing this advancing column of boys and girls sweeping towards them. The field at the bottom of our road was the site for all our bonfires. During the summer it was also the setting for cowboy fights and den making and dangerous expeditions up the railway embankment to place pennies on the line for trains to flatten into shiny lozenges. Now a tall teepee of branches began to take shape, carefully arranged and held together by sheer weight. This bonfire was fiercely guarded and defended from marauding hoards from the other side - the "Leeds Road lot", dangerous ruffians too proud to be bothered chumping for their own bonfire through the inconvenient woodlands and country roads. Their houses sat in treeless streets by the gasworks, I was told. A guard was mounted in the evenings not occupied with homework and boring duties. Some kids had whole bonfires stolen but our magnificent pile escaped the thieving scavengers through the vigilance of our proud and devoted gang.

Bonfire night arrived, with mothers producing tins of home-made parkin and slabs of tooth-breaking toffee, proudly borne on trays down the road. Fathers stood in awe of the sheer size of the mountainous bonfire, not sure whether to stand back or get involved in what seemed to be a well thought out operation, as boys crept proudly about it, poking bits of paper, firelighters and strips of paraffin-soaked rag into the under-pinnings.

The guy, wearing an assortment of strangely recognisable items from our parents' wardrobes, sat helplessly on the top of this magnificent construction wearing a maniacal expression on his papier mâché face, a pipe in his mouth, unaware of the terrible fate which was soon to befall him.

Then the fire was lit, bit by bit. Firelighters were

ignited, briefly giving a sense of achievement as flames zipped and flickered brightly. The wood, being quite damp after overnight rainfall, sulked at first, causing much anxiety among the fathers who stood discussing possible alternative measures. A can was produced. "Stand back!" came the brave command followed by a sudden whoof! as the contents ignited the mountain. Faces lit up as the flames soared towards the guy, still calmly smoking his pipe, but not quite reaching his fragile haven.

Parkin, toffee and mugs of cocoa were distributed as boys got on with the real business of lighting deafening bangers and jumping crackers, unnerving people like my mother who had to go home after five minutes in a state of nervous collapse. Rockets swooshed into the sky and showered stars. Roman candles fired neon coloured balls, beautiful and exhilarating. The dreaded jumping crackers threaded their merciless way amongst the crowd, scattering even the calmest this way and that in giddy fits of shrieks and giggles, not knowing which way they would go next. The guy, resigned to his fate, sank down as if having an evening nap and his pipe melted.

Smoke filled the air with the smell of gunpowder. Sausages arrived and baked potatoes from an oven up the road. Someone brought parkin pigs and gingerbread men with currants for eyes and toffee which glued your teeth together. Finally, Grandpa arrived from Addingham in his brown overalls amid loud cheering from those of us who knew exactly what to expect from his previous year's performance. He walked calmly across to the slowly burning fire, holding large sheets of perforated metal. What could he be doing? wondered the poor uninitiated among us. With a victorious chuckle he tossed the sheets of magnesium onto the fire. White flames shot twenty feet into the air, crackling loudly, and took hold of the whole bonfire, lighting up the sky and the whole valley. Two lads on motor bikes came from over the moor to see what could be causing such a glow in the sky.

The fire burned on and gradually died down, as fireworks, parkin, sausages and cocoa ran out. We stood poking sticks into the furnace, faces smudged and glowing, laughing and talking, planning what we'd do tomorrow ... come down again and make furnaces and cook potatoes ... make charcoal ...

In the run up to Bonfire Night the good people of Ilkley were no strangers to Mischief Night, which happened on the 4th of November and had nothing to do with the witches or turnip lanterns of Halloween.

On this night you were given carte blanche to be as naughty as you liked. We dressed in disguise so that it was difficult for blame to be placed on any particular boy or girl. I got my brother into trouble by wearing a false moustache and one of his old Ghyll Royd school caps. Bangers were put into the letterboxes of front doors and treacle smeared on doorknobs. Boys crouched, sniggering among the laurel bushes while the vicar tried, growling and swearing, to wrench open his front door, the knob of which had been attached by string to the tree in his garden.

People awoke the next morning expecting to find their

garden gate or bicycle gone, usually thrown in the river or down a railway embankment, and helpfully advising each other as to their whereabouts. "Oh, is that your green garden seat in the river? I thought it was!"

The next day was usually spent looking for the missing wheelbarrow or cleaning paint off the sitting room window. Blame was difficult to place on any one individual but some of us were found out and stern words were expressed at school assembly.

Mothers and fathers sighed with relief as another Mischief Night passed and almost looked forward to the letting off of deafening squibs and setting light to the bonfire in the back garden, if it hadn't been stolen, that is.

Christmas at Broadbents

The lights went up on the trees on the Grove far too early, my mother said. Christmas came from nowhere. Suddenly it was time to go to Broadbents and up the stairs into the toy department, to decide what you'd like Father Christmas to bring.

A Hornby Dublo train set lay on the central table, the buzzing train whizzing past painted lead trees sheltering brown and white cows, past the signals, under a bridge and then flicked onto the carpet with a thud. Dolls in boxes stared down from the shelves, mouths red, blue eyes fixed in perfect tearless anticipation. Nurses and soldiers and cowboys. A brown and white spotted rocking-horse in the corner with a white tail, flying white mane and bushy forelock, stirrups and a red bridle and saddle. If only I could have that horse, I wouldn't mind anything if I had that horse. A musical box, Peter Rabbit books, a Plasticene set with ridges of colour smelling of happiness. "Please don't get it on the carpet," the man says. You can make horses out of Plasticene and worms and snakes.

Glitterwax ... and I tell the man that I once made water lilies out of Glitterwax to float in a bowl of water in the garden. The alphabet - A for apple, B for bat, C for cat, D for dog, E for elephant, M for monkey, Z for zebra. A tin musical box with lambs and trees and a handle you can wind up, but please be careful, the man says. "Baa baa black sheep, have you any wool?"

A red pedal car. A fat little boy is howling because he squeezed into it and now can't get out. A xylophone with a little wooden hammer. A kaleidoscope. A detective set with a false moustache and glue, a magnifying glass, a pad for taking fingerprints and a notebook for writing about a burglary in Rupert Road. A gollywog sits on the windowsill with a rabbit. A bear with a sailor hat. Wooden swords and pop-guns and cowboy cap-guns with pearly handles. A water pistol - but the man wouldn't give us any water. Planes with propellers and a yacht with crisp white sails and tiny ropes in coils on the deck.

We have to go now, please, the man says. Down the wooden stairs and into the shop. Atlases and exercise books ... large maps of the world on the wall. A globe that spins. Maps of the Lake District, Somerset, Scotland, Italy and Africa. The Observer's Book of Horses, Battleships, Trains. Beatrix Potter's Peter Rabbit, Enid Blyton's "Five Go on Holiday" and "The Sea of Adventure", Arthur Ransome stories, The Boy Scout's Diary, The Girl Guide Diary, Penguin books, The Bible. Parker and Osmiroid fountain pens, Quink ink, Indian ink, pink blotting paper. Watercolour sketch books and Reeves watercolour sets. Long wooden brushes to wave in the air, pretending to paint. Long fine sable hair brushes to paint eyelashes and a pony's mane and flying tail. Windsor and Newton paints in little lead tubes - cobalt blue, crimson lake, vermillion, yellow ochre. Lakeland Crayons of every colour in the world in a big box that falls onto the floor suddenly, if you are not careful. A wooden easel that smells of the attic. An artist's wooden palette - put your thumb through the hole and paint the sky. I'm going to be an artist, I tell the man.

The man says they're closing now, so we go out and skid along the pavement under the trees and catch snowflakes on our tongues.

Carol singing with the vicar

On the other side of the river large old houses nestled among laurel bushes and tall trees at the ends of winding gravel drives. Ferocious corgis or demented labradors seemed to be the dogs of choice with the residents, so venturing there to sing carols was always a risky operation.

We crunched up the drive carefully, through the dark jungle, to reach a heavy black door. At a signal from the vicar we launched into "Oh, Little Town of Bethlehem", immediately setting off a cacophony of hysterical barking on the other side of the door accompanied by repeated thuds, as heavy dogs threw themselves enthusiastically against it.

The vicar adopted the same facial expression which he reserved for difficult occasions - a manic fixed grin displaying the perfection of ill-fitting National Health dentures as he encouraged us all to keep singing, nodding and conducting us with pale trembling hands.

Then, at a loud roaring command from the other side of the now splintering door frame, the dogs fell silent and scurried away, yelping and whining. A light went on. The door was wrenched open by a large purple-faced gentleman in a red velvet smoking jacket, cigar clenched between teeth and a glass of whisky in his hand.

Behind him was a perfect Christmas scene. A tall Christmas tree with twinkling lights and a fairy in a white net tutu balanced on top, holding a wand with a sparkling star. On the parquet floor below lay the presents, wrapped elaborately with tinsel and red and green ribbons.

He leaned forward, swaying slightly, taking the cigar out of his mouth and surveying us, squinting with bloodshot eyes and smiling like a crocodile. He held out a tightly-folded pound note and squeezed it firmly into the slot of the eagerly held collection tin.

Smiling nervously, the vicar began to thank him but the man, narrowing his eyes and fixing him with a threatening stare, hissed, "Now, bugger orff!" before turning unsteadily and slamming the door.

Christmas dinner

I loved Christmas but my mother loathed and dreaded it as she was expected to sail through it like my father's family, who had it down to a fine art, prepared for weeks ahead and found it a joy. This dread was often enough to put her in bed with a bad back or a headache by the time the dreaded day arrived.

When she was cooking it was as if my mother was being tortured and the stove was the culprit. It was ancient; a 1920s gas stove with a charred black interior which my father had acquired from a bakery in Bradford after it had mysteriously caught fire. It was consequently of a nervous temperament. It had never quite recovered from its terrible ordeal and made loud bangs accompanied by screeching noises and yellow flames when you lit it. On Sundays it would lose power as the rest of Ilkley proceeded to use their perfect gas stoves.

On Christmas morning our expensive and voluptuous turkey sat in the black oven and sulked, refusing to show any signs of cooking at all. It was so large and heavy that it required two people to lift it out for basting. This operation involved a lot scolding and accusations from my mother if you got on the wrong side of the oven or if you giggled or made remarks about the poor pale turkey looking raw. This, accompanied by her moans and yelps of desperation which sent the dog running for cover and my father out into the frosty garden to light his pipe, made for a rather nerve-racking build-up to our much anticipated Christmas dinner.

When we finally sat down at the table, the buxom turkey, now oozing and sizzling smugly in the centre as if nothing was wrong, my mother would announce, sighing, that she thought she had lost her appetite.

But the King's speech was the final straw for her when, at the first drum roll of the National Anthem, my father would suddenly leap to attention, staring through the window into the far distance. Saluting, with gravy dribbling down his chin, a starched napkin and part of the tablecloth tucked into his trousers, he almost carried the whole brave assembly of turkey, vegetables and gravy boat vertically with him.

Skating on the Tarn

I s the Tarn frozen yet? That would be the question we asked as soon as the first feathers of frost streaked the water in the dog's bowl in the garden and old ladies started to slip and fall over on the Grove.

At last word would come. Someone had been up there with their dog, grammar school children had been sliding on it, the ice was safe. Off we would go, dressed in layers of oversized woolly jumpers and our fathers' thick socks, plus scarves, balaclavas and fur gloves, armed with Thermos flasks of hot soup or tea.

It was often night-time when we went, and the moors lay, clad in silent, thick white snow, and shone magically in the silvery blue moonlight. The narrow road snaked up towards the Tarn and as we drew nearer we could hear the scrape of the skates and see the glow of the old Victorian street lamps which bordered the tarn and were lit by a man with a ladder in the early days.

We sat in the wooden shelter and pulled on our skates, lacing them up with already freezing fingers. I learnt to skate in a pair of brown 1920s boots with pointed toes which had belonged to a friend's auntie, now dead. They were size five and I took a size one, so had to wear two pairs of my father's rugby socks.

I slid and staggered across the lumpy ice while more proficient skaters, like the art master Tommy Walker, whistled by with hands in pockets, cigarette in mouth, leaping and turning nonchalantly, going backwards and finishing with a dramatic twirl.

The ducks who lived in a hut on the island in the middle looked on bemused as fluffy-hatted old ladies in long tweed skirts waltzed past, deep in conversation, hands linked, making balletic movements from another era, legs lifted gracefully, arms making patterns in the night sky.

When the cold night air numbed our fingers and toes, we retreated to the shelter to drink our hot tea or Mulligatawny soup and stamp and dance about as the pain of thawing fingers became almost unbearable.

Then, circulation restored, we got back on the ice again, not wanting to miss a moment of the fun, and skate and skate until, clothes wet from falling over, knees bruised, noses blue and fingers numb again, we slid and sledged back down the curving moonlit road to the bottom of the moor. Then it was home to baked beans on toast.

Sometimes the surface of the Tarn became so rough and littered with bits of ice and sticks, or ridged by fresh snowfall, that the fire brigade would have to go up and flood it, restoring the ice to a perfect smoothness, ready for another day.

Art master Tommy Walker on the Tarn

Sledging in Ellis's Field

My sledge, like my brother's, was a sturdy affair made by Grandpa in his workshop, with a thick slab of wood, some iron girders and a piece of knotted rope to lead it. Other kids had streamlined lightweight models, one even with a steering mechanism at the front but ours were built to last way beyond our childhood and were handed down later to any child who didn't laugh at them.

There was a large sloping field just along Skipton Road called Ellis's Field, which was owned by a farmer called Mr Ellis and used for his sheep during the summer. He didn't seem to mind that hoards of people converged on his hill as soon as the snow was deep and hard enough for sledging. We walked along the busy Skipton Road towing an assortment of sledges. Dressed in an assortment of windjammers, woolly jumpers, scarves, balaclavas, gloves and fathers' ex-army jackets, we could have been equipped for an Arctic expedition.

After climbing over the stone wall into the field we launched ourselves down the bumpy slope, feet trailing or up in the air. Amid shouts and screams we plummeted down the steep bumpy slope, heads down, holding onto the front of the sledge for dear life. Noses ran uncontrollably and soon had small icicles dangling from them. Eyebrows and eyelashes acquired a frosty Santa Claus appearance. The fingers of our ice-caked gloves became a useful source of drinking water to be sucked as we climbed back up the hill to start all over again.

Eventually the sheer discomfort and weight of our wet clothes began to take effect and suddenly all we could think of was home and hot soup and a warm fire. A procession of shivering, red-nosed kids walked back along the road, laughing and talking, occasionally chucking snowballs and sliding on sheet ice on the pavement.

Then it was home to the excruciating pain of the circulation returning to fingers and toes, standing in front of a glowing fire on old copies of the Yorkshire Post, wondering what was for tea.

Sunday school

Sunday was a confusing day. You were supposed to like it but nobody seemed very happy. My father dressed in a heavy black coat and set off down the front steps, his shiny black shoes crunching down the path and down the road to church.

Ilkley Parish Church was a dark and frightening place to me, with a loud organ which crashed and wheezed and groaned, sounds so incongruous with nice old God and lambs and angels.

The choir was made up of pink faced boys, giggling and fidgety in white gowns and ruffs, and behind them a row of rather stern men, one of them being my father, whose deep baritone voice boomed out louder than the rest.

The organist, Arthur Pickett, sat leading the choir patiently through hymns and interminable psalms and occasionally went to sleep during the sermon, or nibbled at a bar of Cadbury's milk chocolate which he kept on the side of the keyboard. Arthur had a stammer which fascinated me. One day, when he reached for his chocolate, he found the packet empty and that was the beginning of the great mouse scourge. The organ was found to be inhabited by families of them. They were nibbling bits of the bellows to build their nests, the consequence of which was the occasional embarrassing screech or trumpeting fart midway through "Oh God, our help in ages past" or a solemn funeral march, sending the choirboys into fits of giggles.

Before the service there was an hour of crashing bells, going over and over the same tune, or the same tune backwards, it seemed to me. The biggest, loudest and deepest bell, called Big Tom, was my father's responsibility, as he was the heaviest and strongest of the eight bell-ringers and the only one who could handle it.

The vicar, a bald pointy-headed man with a hooked

The Sunday school with Miss Whitwam in the centre and Diana, front row, second from the left

nose and a rather unattractive temperament, rode full tilt down the road to church on a black bicycle, always late. He fell off, one day and made his nose even worse. With his parrot-like voice, he stumbled and mumbled through the sermon, sometimes forgetting his lines. The choir took the opportunity to have a little snooze.

The Baptist Chapel Sunday School, on the other hand, was a friendly modern-looking place at the bottom of our road. Most children in Ilkley went there, it seemed. Some were from poor families from down by the gasworks who forgot their collection money and some were from more privileged backgrounds who arrived on shiny new bikes. We were all mixed together. The room smelled of a mixture of wet pants, chewing gum, bicycle oil and cough sweets.

Sunday school was overseen by Miss Whitwam, a large fat lady with beady eyes and a small, beak-like mouth, who struck the keys of the upright piano with such zeal that the abundant flesh on her arms bounced about. Miss Whitwam wore her greasy black hair scraped firmly back in a bun, a small ferocious hat pinned to her head with hat pins. Her long dark printed crepe dress did its best to keep in check further mountains of unruly flesh as she hammered the yellowing ivory keys and led us in the opening lines of "Jesus bids us shine, with a pure clear light". This anthem united big and small, rich and poor, who delighted in yelling the final line, "You in your small corner and I in mine!" as loudly as possible. Such a sniffing, coughing, giggling, farting and fidgeting roomful of children might have reduced a lesser mortal to a bundle of nerves, but Miss

Whitwam ruled us with an iron fist. Her word was law and God was on her side.

Required to memorise biblical texts, which were under small beautifully coloured pictures of biblical scenes, then recite them the next week, the majority of children failed miserably, having either lost the texts in pockets full of aniseed balls and conkers or forgotten them.

Every Sunday the dreaded moment arrived. Miss Whitwam made us stand up, one by one, and recite our texts. "Feed My Lambs" was a good one, if you were one of the first in line. "God is Love" was another and "I am the Light" (with a picture of Jesus holding a lantern) was one you could recite fairly safely. I invariably forgot my text so had to make one up. Sometimes it worked, sometimes not. Miss Whitwam had evidently never heard of the "Jesus liked animals" text and I was ticked off severely.

On the walls were large pictures of Jesus, who was blond and handsome with piercing blue eyes and a pale golden skin. I thought that if I had to marry anyone, I'd like to marry him, when I grew up.

Then we had lessons, split into little groups in corners and squeezed into small, wooden chairs. We were read stories from the Bible by a pretty pink-cheeked girl called Winnie Horseman or sometimes by a tall serious young man called Harry Batty who stood for no nonsense. We cut out paper angels and learnt about Moses in the bulrushes, Jesus producing hundreds of fish and loaves out of thin air, Jesus walking on the water and Jesus fishing for more fish. He seemed to be able to do just about anything he liked.

I wondered where he was now, seeing as how he'd got up again after being crucified and I thought that he might like to come to Ilkley one day, if we wrote to him. Harry Batty said not to be silly and that he definitely died in the end, nipping that idea firmly in the bud.

Learning to be small

I started school later than other children because I refused to go. From the first moment that my wrist was grasped firmly by the bony hand of a tall thin whiskery woman in a grey knitted skirt, who smelled of mutton and mothballs, and separated from my little friends and told to "sit here and drink your milk", an escape plan started to form.

After all attempts failed to quell the floods of tears and to silence my loud mournful sobs, a desperate telephone call was made to my mother and I was sent home in a taxi, never to return there again.

I spent a blissful year at home with my beloved mother and the dog and cat, listening to the radio, playing in the garden, painting and drawing and learning to read, until I could go to another school. Moorfield School was run by two very clever and musical sisters, Dorothy and Barbara Thorpe. They lived with their brother Basil and a loud dachshund called Barney in a tall house with a turret among the holly, laurel, beech and fir trees at the foot of Ilkley Moor. Here, the little sons and daughters of wealthy families (except that is for me and a few others) were sent to be taught English, French, arithmetic, geography, history, scripture, general knowledge, nature, gymnastics, tennis, music and art.

The more affluent boys and girls then went on to boarding school and possibly finishing school, married sons and daughters of wealthy families or became professors, artists, writers, singers, drunks or rebels.

The day's assembly started with a bright march, played with determined zeal on an upright piano by Miss Dorothy Thorpe. This music was the signal to bring all five classes of children into the large front classroom, marching solemnly in single file like an orderly army.

Standing with backs straight and heads up, we raised hands as our names were called from the register. On the wall was a large map of a mostly pink world. There were charts of flags and battleships, pictures of Zulus, planets, wildflowers and birds' eggs. Then there was the alphabet with A for Apple, B for Bat, C for Cat, H for Hippopotamus, I for Ink, L for Lion, P for Penguin, T for Tiger, Z for Zebra. The room smelled of Clark's sandals, pencil sharpenings and furniture polish and the sun shone in a bright beam through the bay window onto a large yellowing globe which stood on a table by the marble fireplace.

The BBC had just launched a series of educational programmes for schools, with accompanying booklets, which Miss Thorpe had discovered and used cleverly to ignite and feed the imagination of her pupils. A large wooden radio sat on the mantelpiece. Instead of being bored by the unimaginative ramblings of teachers who had perhaps never been further than Cornwall, we were instead transported into the Amazon jungle, the Himalayas or onto the fishing boats of the North Sea at the turn of a dial.

We heard dramatised sketches of life in China, Argentina, Africa and Birmingham, sailed the high seas at the Battle of Trafalgar and braved the sweaty swamps of the jungle with explorers who, unbeknown to us, were sitting in a stuffy studio in Broadcasting House at the top of Regent Street in London. We learnt about tea growing, coal mining and boat building, jungle insects, blue cheese making and what to do when confronted by crocodiles - all in the large airy room, sitting with hands under chins, eyes far away, enthralled.

In music class we played rather boring percussion instruments - triangles, tambourines, cymbals, castanets and drums. Showing some sense of rhythm, I was picked to conduct and given a baton, which was really a drum stick. We were then entered into the Wharfedale Musical Festival and I was given a proper baton, a beautiful thin wooden wand sent specially from London. It was about half my height and, when taking a break while the triangles were told off or when one of the drums needed a hanky, I stood poking the stick down my knee sock and scratching my leg, a pleasant sensation.

This resulted, to my shame, in it being broken in half which meant a new one had to be sent for at great expense to Miss Thorpe. This happened twice in the lead up to the festival. Almost purple in the face with rage, Miss

Thorpe had to send for another baton, with one week to go before the date we were due to perform. Knee socks were forbidden from then on.

When the big day came I stood in short white socks in front of the audience at the King's Hall. Standing with my back to the audience, facing my eager little band, I raised my baton, stepped back a little - and then a little more.

"Stop!" came a loud command from the adjudicator.

I turned round to see a gentle, white-haired man and hundreds of eager faces, staring up at me.

"My dear!" he pleaded. "Please, please don't step any further back! You are so close to the edge of the stage! A very famous conductor did just what you were doing and fell, breaking his back. He was paralysed for life. I do not want you to meet with the same fate, with your life in front of you."

So I walked away from the edge, took up my new and more boring position, lifted my baton and launched the band into the jolly bouncing tune of "Come Lasses and Lads".

When we were judged the adjudicator said that he had been amused by the enthusiasm of the band, coupled with the conductor's lively movements, and that he'd been unable to stop his feet tapping to the music. We won the first prize.

Mrs Buckmaster

Mrs Buckmaster was an old lady who lived next door but one to us. She was an invalid and sat in an armchair all day. We never asked what was wrong with her, some people were just invalids. She wore hand knitted cardigans and a blouse buttoned up to the neck and had a knitted rug covering her legs, tucked round her to keep the draught out. She sat by the window at a table with a jug of home-made barley water, covered with a small doily with glass beads round the edge to keep the flies out.

As a child I used to go to see Mrs Buckmaster every day, whether she liked it or not. She always seemed delighted to see me and feigned surprise when I knocked on the door. "Who is it?" she called. "Is that Charlie?" to which I shouted "Yes!" as that was my name when I went there.

Sometimes I just rattled the door or made animal noises to frighten her and she was most accommodating, pretending to be terrified. "Oh! Whatever can that be? Is it a wild animal? Halloo!"

Our time was spent engaged in conversation about school. "What did you do today, Charlie?"

"Gym."

"Jim! Jim Fletcher?" (our local greengrocer).

"Nooo! Gym!"

"Ohhh! Gym! Show me what you did!"

Somersaults were performed over the top of the sofa, handstands against the dark patterned wallpaper and doing the crab or crawling under the table if we had been playing "Shipwreck" at the end of term.

Sometimes Mrs Buckmaster was in bed in the sitting room. This did not spare her from taking part in our adventures and the bed became a stagecoach being driven across a prairie, chasing Red Indians. I sat at the foot of the bed, whipping the horses with a walking stick and firing at Indians with it as well. We thundered across canyons and had to fight off bandits and wild animals. Mrs Buckmaster's energy seemed to know no bounds and she spurred me on, shouting "Go on, Charlie! Faster!"

Sometimes I was required to read to her from The Dalesman magazine when it arrived each month, in a broad Yorkshire accent, a poem called Young Fred. It featured a scruffy farm lad sitting on a wall, talking about his exploits in the Dales. Mrs Buckmaster sat, hand to mouth to suppress her laughter, her eyes sparkling, until I finished and then she would applaud and chuckle.

One afternoon in the middle of Young Fred, she started to stare straight ahead, gasping loudly and rocking back and forth. Thinking it was one of her jokes but a little frightened, I tried to carry on reading but then dropped the book and, terrified, opened the back door and ran home. My mother went to investigate. Mrs Buckmaster had had a seizure and was dead.

A day trip to Morecambe

The trains which came through Ilkley took people to the Lake District and to Scotland (changing at Skipton) and, most importantly, to the seaside. We skipped along to the station, a raucous band of eager children marshalled by Iris, the nanny whose voice could rise above them all like a bugle on a battlefield, and a willing aunt.

We bundled into the dusty old carriage and onto the prickly seats. Our buckets and spades, fishing nets, towels and bags of "sangwidges" were put up onto the brown net luggage rack above framed scenes of highland cattle, lakes, mountains and sandy bays.

The noise of this little tribe of children reached such a pitch that the stationmaster could hardly be heard as he yelled, "Morecambe train!" The porters ambled up the platform, closing the heavy doors with a slam.

Then, after a screech from the whistle, the whole train lurched forwards and with a deep puff from the engine we were off. Iris, whose voice was the only one ever to rise above those of her charges, commanded us all to sit down, but this fell on deaf ears as we surged to the window and looked out upon our Ilkley from this very strange angle. We floated across the iron bridge, over Brook Street, peering through the struts at the people shopping. Yelling and pointing at familiar landmarks, we marvelled at being able to see behind the Grove Cinema and the shops, which all looked quite undignified with ugly dark windows. WH Smiths and Broadbents, Eileen Walker the ladies' hairdresser and Miss Graham's posh children's outfitters, all took on a rather dull, grim appearance when viewed from the rear.

*A locomotive pulling out of Ilkley Station
and crossing Brook Street over the iron bridge*

Our excitement grew as we came nearer to the Crawfords' house near the railway embankment and the sight of it caused wild delight and deafening shouts of joy, much to the horror of the Outhwaites, their long suffering next door neighbours, who scuttled inside. A shout of "Mrs Ouuuuthwaite!!!" rent the peaceful air of Westville Road, lowering the tone, before the train galloped across the arch of the sooty millstone grit bridge and carried the rowdy hoard safely away up the valley towards the sea.

Our thoughts turned to the sandwiches nestling seductively out of reach above our heads and, although Iris ruled with a rod of iron, by the time we had gone past Skipton her resistance was being tested severely. She had to physically restrain the loudest, strongest child and pacify her with a Fox's glacier mint, plucked out of her supply which hid in the depths of her plastic handbag.

At last we arrived at Morecambe. Rather like a scene from an old St Trinian's film, we surged noisily out of the station, waving our spades, and descended down the steps onto the sandy beach. Hours were spent digging holes and filling them with water, riding donkeys and eating sandy sandwiches. Then came the terrifying ride on the Big Dipper and an even more frightening journey through the dark cobwebby tunnels of the ghost train. Ice cream and candy floss finally quietened this rowdy band.

Exhausted, we piled onto the train, wet cozzies and towels in bags, sand in our sandals, our hair and everywhere else. When the train finally approached Ilkley, we leaned out of the window, cheering to see once more our beloved

moors and the dull backs of the shops and the Grove
Cinema ... and poor Mr and Mrs Outhwaite prepared for a
return to the normality of a less peaceful life.

Riding school

The girls at my first school, run by the Thorpe sisters, were all pony mad. Some of them had ponies of their own which were often liveried at the local stables next to the Lister Arms.

At break time girls pretending to be ponies galloped and whinnied across the grassy playing field next to the school,

The riding school, led by Ken Hampshire,
with Diana, the smallest rider, on a
piebald pony on the right

reined up with long pieces of string or driven by holding onto long plaits or cardigan sleeves. They were groomed with handfuls of grass and urged onwards by the wielding of long twigs.

Although Sarah Day's rearing and whinnying were very convincing and she did have very long plaits, there was still the aching need for the real thing. After numerous occasions when haughty girls rode past our garden gate on their way to the moors, my pleas for riding lessons became too much and my mother managed to persuade my father. Six shillings would have to be found and a lot more for jodhpurs. These were found at a country gentlemen's outfitters in Skipton, the market town. They were made from sturdy brown corduroy, not the slim fitting tailor-made beige ones worn by the snooty girls going past the gate. These were rather baggy and the legs were too long so had to be turned up at the bottom. My brother laughed but they were jodhpurs and smelled wonderful.

The first riding lesson started with the allocation of suitable mounts. I was given the smallest pony, a sturdy brown and white animal called Bonny who had an air of bored resignation and carried me carefully round the stable yard. We trotted, rising up and down in the saddle, to calls of, "Knees in! Feet in! Heels down! Heads up! Backs straight!"

We then set off across the main road and down towards the river. It felt like the first day of my life. If I had known then that people pinched themselves when something seemed unbelievable, that is what I would have done.

In an orderly line, we walked to a field by the river, had a few more lessons in trotting and stopping (harder than I had imagined, as Bonny did not like stopping) and then on past the cricket club and along the road by the river.

As we trotted, Ken the instructor sang a little song;

"I've got a pretty little black eyed pony,
Jig, jog, jig, jog, jigga jog jee,
Not too fat and not too bony,
Jig jog jig jog jigga jog jee,
We go riding merrilee,
I love her and she loves me, etc"

Which I thought just about did it, no snobbishness, just happy to be alive. He was a human being. He rolled his sleeves up, smoked a cigarette and had twinkling blue eyes. I was in love.

We trotted back over the bridge and across the main road to the stables. I walked home, tapping my leg with my crop, humming the little song and down the garden path, beaming.

The next week at school I said I'd been riding. "Oh, which pony did you ride?" asked Lukie (whose real name was Elizabeth). She was almost as small as me.

"Bonny!" I said proudly.

"Oh, that's my pony," she said, turning her nose up slightly.

"Oh, she's lovely!" I effused.

"She's going to be sold soon," said Lukie, flatly.

The following week Bonny shied at a barking dog, throwing me over her head into the road. Then she turned and thundered with her little hooves over my upturned chest, knocking the wind out of me and leaving a hoof print on my ribs for weeks.

The Miss Inglebys

At the end of the road, just by the red post box, there was a beech hedge and a high wall which enclosed a long sloping garden leading up to a large stone house. Here lived the Miss Inglebys, as we called them. They were spinsters. There were a lot of spinsters in Ilkley. My mother told me that it was perhaps because they had been "disappointed in love" or that some of them had "lost someone during the war" as many had.

The Miss Inglebys seemed to be very content to live together without husbands. In fact the intrusion of male company, although politely entertained, would have been an interruption to their idyllic existence.

Children, on the other hand, were treated with great respect and spoken to as adults, being encouraged to engage in long complicated conversations and invited to take tea beside the lawn. So it was to this refuge that I sometimes wandered on summer afternoons, quite alone.

There was a large dark green wooden gate in the high wall with a heavy latch which made a sound like a gun, announcing my arrival to the small dogs hitherto fast asleep somewhere under the trees, setting them barking and bouncing in a feathery way, as long-haired dachshunds do. "Ah! There you are, my dear!" would be my unconditional welcome, as though they had been wondering where I was and had just discovered me.

We sat at a small bamboo table under the trees, listening to the wood pigeons, while tea was poured into china cups and there were small sandwiches of meat paste and iced buns. I noticed that the birds seemed to be completely without fear and hopped about, waiting for crumbs.

"What would you like to be when you grow up?" asked the smaller Ingleby sister, leaning forward and looking me in the eye.

"I think she has the spirit of adventure!" the other sister chimed. "A true explorer!"

"I'd like to be an artist," I announced solemnly "and have a horse." Then, for good measure and suddenly remembering my true goal in life, I added, "And go on stage and be an impressionist." Then I launched into my impression of a creaking door.

This revelation seemed to make them search for other things for me to do. "Imagination! Imagination is the key!" whispered the tall sister, handing me a jam tart. "Use it, dear! You have the gift!"

"My Uncle Jack is on the stage in Morecambe," I went on. "He impersonates people. He can do Al Jolson and Max Wall!" Fearing the approach of an Al Jolson impression to spoil the calm of a summer afternoon, the smaller of the two sisters had an idea. "Do you play tennis, dear?" she asked, waving a hand towards the lush green court.

"I'm not very good," I said. "At school I hit a girl with

my racquet by mistake and she had to go home."

Much to my relief this seemed to amuse the sisters, at the same time putting them off the idea.

So we went exploring in their vast jungle of a garden, accompanied by barking dogs and the sudden inclusion of a giant grey cross-eyed Persian cat. I showed them how Tarzan swung on trees and grazed my knee. At my request one of the sisters made a posy of wild roses, forget- me-nots and dandelions to take home to my mother.

"You must come again, dear," they would say, rather relieved as I left through the big green gate. And I always did.

Art lessons with Miss Heaps

At the top of the Avenue opposite our house lived two old ladies, Miss Heaps and Miss Oddie. Miss Heaps was an artist who later told me tales of when she had trained in Paris in the 1920s. She then went to Leeds College of Art and was a friend of the famous "Mr. Owen Bowen," as she called him.

When I was nine someone suggested to my mother that I should be sent to Miss Heaps for lessons, as I already showed some ability. The fee was two shillings and sixpence.

Arriving for my first lesson one Saturday morning, I reached up and rang the bell. Some time elapsed then there was some scuffling and tremulous murmuring behind the door and the sound of a key being turned. The door was wrenched open by a tiny frail creature in a long cardigan, who clung to the handle as if it were her only means of support. Then, risking all, she threw her hands in the air and said, "Ah! Oh! My dear! Do come in! Come in!" Turning, she led me down a long dark hallway and into a bright sunny room full of framed pictures of animals, flowers and landscapes. Cats, dogs, horses and birds and a rather cross

Diana's pastel painting of a horse

looking guinea pig all stared down at me from the wall. "And here," she said, smiling to the audience and sweeping a bony hand theatrically towards me, "is Diana!" Then, leaning forwards, almost in a whisper, she said, "My dear, I have been expecting you! Oh yes! Indeed!"

She spoke in bursts of sound, as if someone was squeezing her. "My dear, do have a seat. Would you like some tea?"

Quite dazzled by all this, I nodded and said that I would and she disappeared for a moment. I stood listening to murmurings in the hall, transfixed by a large chestnut horse with a pale golden mane whose brown eyes seemed to be looking straight down at me from its frame on the wall.

When Miss Heaps came back she smiled, revelling in my look of enchanted amazement. "Ah, yes!" she said, "You are an animal lover of course. Some of these are very, very old friends. Some, sadly, are no longer with us but, as you see, they are still very much alive! Do look around, my dear!"

Looking at the horse, I reached out and touched it. The paper was soft and furry - my first introduction to pastel painting.

"Ah! I know you are fond of animals. Your mother has told me that you ride, as did I when I was young, in the country."

Seeing my attachment to the horse she leaned forward. "Have no fear! We will paint him! Yes, we will, my dear! But first, perhaps, we will begin with a little charcoal drawing!"

She produced some long black twigs and I said that I liked making charcoal from the wood from the bonfires we had on our waste land. This information was accepted as perfectly normal and we went to work on a drawing of a small upturned plant pot and a china rabbit. I was shown how to hold the charcoal between my thumb and fingers, a strange thing to do, for me. I found this rather boring.

Suddenly there was the rattling of crockery and a tinkling of spoons, followed by a discreet knocking. Miss Heaps flew to the door like a small bird.

"And this is Miss Oddie! With the tea, Come in, dear!" Then, turning to me, she said, "Would you like a cup of tea, my dear?"

I nodded enthusiastically, noticing with fascinated interest that Miss Oddie seemed to have a moustache.

"And a biscuit? They are very good!"

I just sat there, nodding and smiling, in this room full of sunshine and animals. Tea was poured into china cups from a teapot in a blue knitted tea cosy. I was given a fragile bone china plate, painted with forget-me-nots, and handed delicate home-made ginger biscuits.

"My dear," whispered Miss Oddie as if we were in church, "do you take sugar?" I nodded, hypnotized by the moustache.

"One lump, or two?" asked Miss Heaps, smiling and brandishing the silver tongs as if conducting an orchestra.

"Oh, one, please." We sat silently, stirring tea and smiling, eating ginger biscuits. Outside, it began to rain and then hail, beating against the bay window. I was staring at the horse. "We shall paint him, my dear," beamed Miss Heaps, leaning forward and looking me in the eye. "Have no fear. We shall! We shall! But first, perhaps I should introduce you to this little fellow." She reached for a small framed portrait of a Siamese cat, its perfect, sapphire blue eyes beaming back at me from dark brown rims and a creamy, pale face.

Her own tiny face tilted to one side, Miss Heaps looked at me and asked, "Would you like to paint him?" Then, with an air of conspiracy, she leaned forward, holding a

Tea with Miss Heaps

fragment of sapphire blue pastel and whispered, "Shall we see what fun we shall have with him?" And she passed me another ginger biscuit.

It is hard to resist an opportunity to venture into the unknown when faced with the confident smile of an eighty-two-year-old lady offering more tea and biscuits.

Dilly Dell's boats

Down by the river, below the Old Bridge, where the big old trees leaned and trailed their heavy branches over the sweet-smelling water, swallows caught flies in the air, midges hovered in clouds and trout hid among slippery brown stones, were Dilly Dell's boats.

He had ten beautiful but rickety old rowing boats which sat creaking in the water, tied like horses with long ropes to the stone landing stage, shifting now and then with the river breeze. They each had a number and some had faintly painted names - Rita, Mona, Rose.

Further down the river, a weir made of large stones and boulders kept the water level just high enough for Dilly's boats to be rowed up and down without catching their bottoms on the river bed, or going completely aground.

At the weekend the river was busy with boats. Young sailors on leave, showing off their newly acquired skills, took their girlfriends for a leisurely trip down the water. They would end up, more often than not, moored in the cool dappled shade of a big overhanging tree, wrapped in a precarious and passionate embrace, gazing into each other's eyes.

Dilly Dell's boats

Young lads tried their hand at rowing, laughing, "catching crabs" and ramming each other just for fun while older men were more graceful and dignified, seeming to make the oars float through the water without a sound.

Mr Dell, or Dilly Dell as he was known, was a jolly, thick-set soft-eyed old man with a grey, bushy, nicotine-stained moustache, twinkling eyes, a big generous grin and a fascinating amount of hair in his ears. He wore a sailor's navy peaked cap and a big cream cable-knit sailor's jumper over baggy blue trousers tucked into heavy wellington boots.

He talked of dreams of grand projects which he seemed to have an urgent need to share with us girls and boys, whether we were interested or not. He was so confident about these projects that no one had any doubt that they would succeed. One of his dreams was to put on a huge concert in the playing fields on the opposite bank of the river where well known entertainers would perform in front of hundreds of people, backed by a symphony orchestra and brass bands. Even the Queen was included in his list of possible visitors to these events, as well as Roy Rogers and Trigger, Vera Lynn, the Pope, Billy Graham and Arthur Askey. It was no use scoffing or questioning the viability of these extravaganzas because he would just look at you with pity, as if you had no real understanding of what was possible in this world.

Our small gang hung about on Dilly's jetty at the weekends, helping him with the boats in the blind hope that one day, as he kept promising, we could have a free ride. "Free rides tomorrow!" he would say. So the next day we would turn up, only to be told with a chuckle, "Ah, but I said, free rides tomorrow!"

One year, nearing the beginning of the boating season, Dilly presented us with a proposition. We would rebuild his weir with rocks and he would provide the boat, or maybe two, for us to carry out this operation. We must collect big stones from just below the Old Bridge and carry them in one or maybe two of his oldest leakiest boats down to the broken down weir and build it up, ready for the new season.

We were hardly able to believe what we'd just heard. Afraid that he might change his mind if we showed too much enthusiasm, we agreed in the most nonchalant manner we could muster.

The next day five of us rowed up the river in the leakiest old boat, Rita, number ten, to just below the Old Bridge. We stood in the water and heaved huge mossy stones into the bottom of the boat with a heavy thud. Surprisingly, Rita's bottom held out and then, propelled by a rather novel mixed style of rowing, she bravely bore this load down to the weir, gradually filling up with a certain amount of water as she went. She had a tendency to veer to the left, almost decapitating the crew with overhanging tree branches or, more interestingly, to turn completely round and go backwards, depending on the combined skills of whoever was rowing at the time.

At the weir we piled out into the water in bare feet and gradually unloaded the cargo, building up the collapsed parts of the weir, slipping about painfully on the mossy stones on the river bed, laughing and talking, getting wet in the warm sunshine. When we had run out of rocks we went back up to the bridge, loaded up more then came back down and continued standing in the water.

Suddenly one day, catching sight of something glinting in the water on the river bed, a girl reached down and, with a cry of surprise, held something up. It was a little gold statuette, dripping and sparkling in the sunlight - a Buddha, although we didn't know it at the time.

"Gold! It's gold!" we cried, like all the good pirates we'd read about.

"A burglar must have thrown it in the water when he was being chased by the police!" said one. Or, I said, it might have been thrown over the bridge by a jilted sweetheart. Nobody thought that was a good idea at all.

"I bet it's worth hundreds of pounds!" said one boy who knew about these things, adding, darkly, "We could sell it!"

This idea seized the imagination and we forgot about the weir for a while and set about gazing into the water, shifting small stones with our feet, lifting bigger stones together, searching for more treasure.

There, glinting in the deep water, was another Buddha. This one had a different hat, taller and more pointed, a serene smile on its face. We carried on searching, hoping for more, but there were none. Now we were afraid to keep them. What if they'd been stolen? We'd be found out and arrested!

"Don't be daft," said one rather knowledgeable boy,

"they don't put children in prison." Then he added, as if to reassure us, "Our parents'll probably go to prison."

Faced with this horrifying prospect, one of the gang wrapped them up in a large rather dirty hanky, took them up to the police station and we never heard anything of them again.

After about a week, the weir restored to its original height, we had to return our beloved leaking boats and go back to being a nuisance again.

Guide Camp

The 2nd Ilkley Guide Company met in a hot stuffy room near the boiler belonging to the Wells Road Methodist Church. It was a very old company, having been formed in 1915. We found some old 1920s navy felt guide hats in a cupboard and adopted them as our alternative uniform. They came in particularly handy at our annual guide camp, fending off rain and, in the unusual

The 2ⁿᵈ Ilkley Guides preparing for a camping adventure, with Diana centre front

event of bright sunshine, shading the eyes. We pulled them right down over our eyebrows and pulled faces, like the Goons.

Rain, howling gales and flooded tents were the requisite conditions for character building and these were in plentiful supply at most camps, especially one in the Lake District where a stream flowed through my tent and I went home.

We would set off in Forrest's removal lorry, leaning out and cheering and waving to everyone, like something out of a St Trinian's film, as we were driven through Ilkley and off to the mystery location. One year, after quite a long journey, we arrived at Howick, Northumberland.

For some strange reason, the sun was shining. Wood pigeons were cooing continually in the tall trees, other birds sang and the fire stayed alight instead of sulking and smouldering. We could walk about in shorts and short sleeves.

One day we took a walk through the woods on the side of the site which opened onto an idyllic beach where gentle waves lapped around the rocks. On the rocks were hundreds of winkles. I knew about winkles. We ate them when we went to Morecambe and they were delicious. I told the others, "We can boil them and eat them, using the pins on our badges to pick them out."

With this in mind, they started to collect them from the rocks, putting them in their berets or anything else handy. I boiled them up in a big pan of salt water back at camp and we sat and ate them with great relish, using our badge pins. They really were a great success, I thought, until the middle of the night when there seemed to be a lot of loud activity in the first aid tent. Torches were being shone as relays of stretchers carrying pale retching and groaning bodies went to and fro in the darkness. We learnt later that you mustn't collect winkles in a month with no R in it, so July was obviously a mistake. The strange thing is, no one in my tent suffered at all.

Johnny Brown

Johnny Brown is dead. He was killed, driving his big car. In his early days at school his brilliant mind separated him from some of the others in the B form. He lived in a world of cowboys, gangsters and Teddy boys. His father owned a string of cinemas so he saw a lot of films. His face was like a character from a cartoon with sad eyes, eyebrows that expressed his every emotion, a protruding chin and a sad mouth which could break suddenly into a broad grin.

One day in art class we were given a subject on which to base our composition and waited eagerly to start. Johnny Brown always managed to position himself next to me until we were eventually separated for our own good because he made me laugh and kept asking me to marry him.

Mr Walker gave us "The Picnic" as the title for that particular morning's class. An innocent enough subject, you might think. For Johnny Brown, though, "The Picnic" turned out to be a scene of violent carnage with cowboys sitting round, eating and drinking beer and shooting each other and the odd Indian letting fly with an arrow which stuck into the chest of a cowboy, mid-sandwich. It was a weird composition built with vile green, blood red and electric blue, purple and yellow and a lot of black.

The men in the painting had huge scars on their faces with big stitches, Desperate Dan chins stuck with stubble, Teddy boy haircuts, quiffs and sideburns. Cigarettes hung luxuriously from mean mouths, knives gleamed in hairy fists, guns poked from pockets and rope nooses dangled from lamp posts.

The next week Mr Walker came up with what he thought was a foolproof idea. "The Village Green," he sighed, in the vain hope that some change in perception might have occurred miraculously in Johnny's mind since the previous week. But a maypole has many uses, apparently, and Johnny's idea of gay ribbons were thick bands of coloured rope, knotted round unfortunate Teddy boys' necks in various stages of strangulation. They whirled horizontally round the pole, watched by policemen and cowboys unless they themselves were shooting each other, being bitten by giant mad dogs or coshed by other policemen.

As I sat next to him Johnny was giving me a whispered running commentary on what was happening. "An' then there's this Ted, yer see, an' e's got a flick knife, an' it goes 'Urgghh!' into this man's face, with all blood an' guts comin' out an' 'e goes, 'Urgghh!' an' 'e falls in the gutter an' 'is face is all pale, an' there's all guts comin' out."

He was hunched over the paper, seeing everything vividly, as if it were a film. At one point he leaned over to me, his chin jutting out like Desperate Dan's with a charming conspiratorial grin from ear to ear, and whispered, "I've run out of blood. Can I have some of your red?"

"Only if you wash your brush first," I began but it was too late. The murky brush had done its worst, dirtying up my clean colours before going on its way, splishing and sploshing ghastly tracks of curdled blood onto the severed arm of an already anaemic- looking gangster.

When our work was pinned on the wall at the end of the class much of Johnny's painting became a landslide of colour which gradually slid off the paper and ended with a plop on the studio floor.

A few years later, I bumped into Johnny one evening at a bus stop in Leeds when I was going home from Art College. He was in awe when I told him I was now an art student. His eyes lit up and he asked, "Are you a beatnik?"

He looked extremely neat and smart. I asked him where he was working and he told me he had a very responsible management job at the Grand Hotel, with prospects of promotion.

"Marvellous!" I said. "Do you like it?"

He looked at me with his big, funny face and smiled sadly.

"It's not much fun," he said.

Rock 'n' Roll Club

It is the early 1950s and rock 'n' roll is grabbing the attention of all the young people in Ilkley. We buy records at Allen and Walker where the bewildered proprietor looks puzzled and asks, "Be-bop a what?" and Radio Luxembourg crackles and fades on our old walnut veneer radio, on which you can still get Hilversum and Moscow. Little Richard screams "A wop bop aloobop, a wop bam boom!" and my mother gets very cross and turns him off, hoping he will go away.

I am thirteen. I am not, she says, under any circumstances going to be allowed to go to any Rock and Roll Club, even if my precocious little school friend Jackie is going. Jackie wears her big sister's push-up bras and has very long eyelashes.

Down the quiet leafy road from our house, under the railway bridge and across the main road, stands an elegant broad-fronted hotel called The Ilkley Moor where Rotary Club dinner dances are held. In the smoky private bar slouch young chaps in cavalry twill trousers, clutching pint tankards to their chests, smoking pipes and discussing cars and cricket, guffawing loudly. A golden Labrador snoozes by the open fire. An elegant tanned woman in a tweed skirt and cashmere twin-set is perched on a tall stool, cigarette holder in one hand, gin and tonic in the other, discussing her recent holiday in the South of France with an enthralled barman.

Meanwhile, round the side of the hotel in the small elegant ballroom above the vaults, Ilkley Rock 'n' Roll Club opens its doors for the very first time. The town will never be quite the same again.

Splitting the quiet night air, the sound of Little Richard hollering "Tutti Frutti" filters through the tall trees and dripping laurel bushes outside and sends spotty, rubber legged boys in suede, crepe-soled shoes and drainpipe trousers flying onto the polished dance floor. Boys with cockscomb quiffs and DA haircuts, Brylcreemed and sculpted to stay put, throw skinny girls in cheap perfume and tight skirts over their shoulders, between their legs, twirling and jumping, cigarettes dangling nonchalantly from their mouths.

Girls with lacquered beehive hairdos, pointed bras under tight sweaters, waspie belts and skirts too tight to walk in, black eyeliner flicked up in wings and shiny Italian pink lipstick. Girls with Audrey Hepburn urchin haircuts in black ballerina pumps, slick, bare legs whirling frothy net petticoats under circles of black taffeta, round and round, lifting high in the air, faces set in concentration.

Eunice Goff, tall and thin like Olive Oyl, and John Cartwright take the floor and perform lightning steps, he with his head flicking from side to side with the music as

Rock 'n' roll beats a path to Ilkley

he throws her over his shoulder and emerges with a rubber-legged leap, then spins her out and reels her in like a yo-yo.

Then there's a fight. The music stops. Heavy thumps in a corner of the room. Girls scream and run for the ladies toilets. A thin boy in a white nylon shirt, blood pouring from his nose, walks slowly away, turning with threats and is led off by a tearful girl. A breathless overweight hall porter, navy hat in hand, looks relieved as he arrives just a bit too late.

The music plays on. "Weell, Be- Bop a loo la! She's mah Bay-beh!" and a tall blond lad with a lot of festering spots, white nylon shirt and crew cut, suddenly stands in front of me, arms dangling, grinning and asking me to dance. Afraid and shy, I shake my head and say no, I don't know how.

My brother sees me and says. "Go on, you'll be alright!"

The boy holds out his big, surprisingly wet hands. Suddenly I'm being whirled around and pulled in, expertly manipulated, twirled and squeezed, intoxicated by the overpowering bitter smell of stale sweat. I have to hold my breath.

"Ye're alright!" he says, holding me and whirling me until I'm dizzy.

Suddenly I am whisked away, stolen by Doik the butcher's lad who has been drinking and has a very different style, sinuous and gently seductive, dangerous. He slouches and slides in his black suede crepe-soled shoes, a long pale blue jacket floating with him as he takes my hand, holds me tight and dances. He buries his face in my neck, as Fats Domino sings, "Ah ... found ... mah .. .thrill ... orn Blueberry Hill."

A little later it's time to go. I have to be home by nine-thirty, my mother had said. Reluctantly I get my coat and go outside where there are boys hanging about with girls, smoking and kissing among the dark laurel bushes.

To my horror, out on the wet pavement by one of these dark laurel bushes is my mother with our dog, which is pulling on the lead, trying to investigate a couple snogging passionately and dangerously behind it.

"Well! I've never seen such goings on!" she says as she steers me firmly away. "It's the last time you come here, my girl!" And I am escorted home.

A few weeks later, having read about the cinema seats being torn out at showings of "Rock Around the Clock" in various towns throughout England, the sensible manager of the Grove Star Cinema has the first three rows of the stalls removed and invites members of Ilkley Rock 'n' Roll Club to come and dance to the music.

We all go, and whenever the music starts we get up and dance, much to the surprise of the rest of the audience. Then, suddenly Doik, the butcher's lad, gets up onto the narrow stage in front of the screen and does a slow, graceful, rubber-legged solo, bending backwards to touch the floor, silhouetted by the projector's beam. Even the people in the dress circle stand and applaud.

Going home from school

Going home from school
On a snowy winter's evening ...
The steep road from the moors
Filled with loud voices, laughing
And indignant yells and screams
As boys scoop snow off walls
And pelt girls in bottle green macs
Or passing cars as they clink up the road,
Their tyres in chains ...
Snow blows sideways in the street lamplight,
Pausing gracefully, mid-air
Then whirling away in a spiral,
Caught in the headlights,
Not looking cold at all but suddenly golden.
Feet starting to numb again,
Cold inside fur boots,
Not quite dried out on the radiators
From the morning ...

The warm light of Ilkley Station
And the heavy thud, thud, of the engine
As it pulls out,
Bound for Ben Rhydding,
Burley in Wharfedale, Menston, Guiseley.
Pink faces of boys at the windows,
Suddenly serious ...
No more jostling and fighting ...
Home for baked beans on toast,
Homework to be handed in tomorrow,
Latin, maths, history ...
Watching Dad smoke his pipe and
Read the evening paper,
While steam rises from the
Damp socks by the fire.

The bathing pool

The Ilkley outdoor pool was the centre of activity for us all summer. Rain or shine, we spent all our spare time there. A season ticket cost ten shillings and the water was never less than icy cold, even on the hottest day. We swam even when it was raining and withdrew, teeth chattering and blue with cold, to the café at the end of the green, manicured lawns for scalding hot Bovril and Smith's crisps.

I inherited my brother's navy wool Jantzen swimming costume which had embarrassing little legs and clung heavily when wet, drooping and dripping, to my blue body. The white rubber swimming cap snapped, cruelly onto one's head, causing a permanent frown, constricting the eyebrows and making all attempts at communication from anxious mothers very difficult.

So, frowning and shivering, weighed down by my dripping swimming costume, I would bravely re-enter the shallow end and try, once more, to swim. There was a certain amount of mockery from my little friends who, encouraged by ambitious mothers and shiny two shilling pieces, had already mastered the art of staying afloat and not drowning

Bronzed bodies and bikinis round the pool

and now cavorted noisily in the luxurious blue buoyancy of the deep end. I stayed with one foot on the bottom for what seemed like weeks, hopelessly floundering and swallowing a considerable amount of chlorinated water. Then I discovered that I had no difficulty swimming underwater. This became my preferred mode of action, zooming like a fish out of view, to the alarm of a friend's mother who feared I had drowned.

The pool was managed by Mr and Mrs Hatch, a handsome couple. Mr Hatch had a serious bronzed face and sparkling blue eyes, like Alan Ladd, and his wife had blonde hair wound round her head in plaits. She had a perfect Grace Kelly figure and moved with grace, in and out of the water. Between them they managed the changing cubicles and kept strict order at all times, putting up with no rowdy behaviour or towel flicking from anyone.

As we got a bit older, we sunbathed on the lawns, applying Nivea and developing deep tans. The boys, their muscles gleaming, strutted about, snapping their satin swimming trunks and combing their hair in Tony Curtis quiffs and DA's and dived from the high boards to impress the girls, as well as each other.

We discovered that olive oil, bought only from Boots and costing two shillings, gave us a lovely golden tan, even better if mixed with vinegar but making you smell like a salad dressing, although salad dressing was unheard of in our house.

I made my own very brief bikini from a scrap of dark striped cotton tie material, found in the attic and re-

The Ilkley outdoor pool was the place to be in summer
Diana is at the back in the pale swimsuit and her
cousin Rod Hewitt is on the left at the front

enforced with small whalebone strips. This outfit stayed up even when diving or doing handstands. My mother complained that it was not decent and that was all the approval I needed. I had very little to put inside a bra but its shape went ahead without me and it was an instant success.

Cliff Richard at the pool

It was another scorching hot day down at Ilkley swimming pool and I was "swotting" with two friends for German GCE the following day. We lay on the lawn on towels in our bikinis, applying sun lotion now and then. Suddenly one sat upright and said, "It's 'im!"

"Who?"

"Him! Cliff Richard! 'E were on t' telly last night! 'E's a new discovereh. It's 'im!"

She pointed a pearlised pink nail towards the café veranda where three men were sitting at a table. I was still none the wiser as commercial television hadn't yet reached Ilkley.

"Come on, let's go an' walk past 'im to the café!" said Sue, who was a bit more daring when it came to men. "We can get an ice lolly! Come on!"

After a lot of fixing make-up and hair and adjusting bikini-bottoms, we got up and walked nonchalantly past the three men at the table, pretending to be deep in conversation in German.

They watched silently as we returned, sucking orange lollipops, and as we passed one of them called out, "Hello!

Hi! Guten Tag! Wie geht's?" This was something we had not expected and we stopped mid-lolly, mouths ajar.

"Guten Tag!" we chorused and then giggled. He asked us something in German we couldn't understand so we came clean. "Oh, we're not really German!" I said.

Cliff's manager introduced himself and we all shook hands with Cliff, asked for his autograph and he signed the back of my season ticket with my "Italian Pink" lipstick. He signed my daring friend's bare back with her "Sweet Tangerine" lipstick.

Then the manager spoke up. "Cliff would like to go swimming but he's too shy to go in on his own. Would you help us out and come in with him?" So we did. Cliff stood shyly on the pool surround.

"Maybe all jump in at once!" came the command from his manager. So we did, taking a run at it and causing a lot of splashing. I was just coming to the surface when I was suddenly pushed under again, two hands firmly gripping my shoulders, sending me down into the deep water. Panicking, I struggled for my life and rose to the surface, coughing and choking, coming face to face with Cliff. Full of remorse he helped me to the side where I clung for dear life to the ledge, gasping for breath. "I'm not a strong swimmer!" I wheezed, apologetically.

"I am so sorry! I didn't realise!" he shouted over the squeaks and splashes of the other bathers. He stayed with me as we held on to the side and trod water, talking. He asked me if I lived in Ilkley and said how lucky I was. He didn't leave my side until he was sure I was alright. Close up,

I suddenly saw how young he was, still in his adolescence.

Afterwards we all stood on the surround in the sunshine, watching people and talking. Girls came up and asked him for his autograph. Later I got ready to go home and was just walking outside the fence when a big open American car pulled up alongside, with Cliff and his managers inside.

"We'd like you to come to the show tonight in Harrogate, as Cliff's guest. Will you come?"

I said I couldn't as I had the GCE German exam in the morning and anyway, it would be difficult to get a bus back to Ilkley late at night. "Ah well! What a shame!" they said and drove off, Cliff waving and smiling.

Dangerous boys at the Saturday dance

Haggis, Doik, and Ginner
Names to drive parents mad,
At the mere mention ...
Boys who swaggered onto the dance floor,
Grabbed you by the wrist
And took you over ...
Shameless confidence of style,
Conversationless except for
Whispered dangerous propositions,
Between the twizzles of the bop ...
With heads flying sideways,
Feet that flew in circles,
Weighed down by blue suede shoes
And shoulders
Where their shoulders weren't,
Suspending long jackets in gentle pastels,
Flecked with black or white, or silver.
With tousled, effortless charm
They reeled you in and
Played you out ...
And never let you go.

A group of Ilkley lads including Diana's brother Ian in the back row, third from the right, and Doik, the rubber legged dancer, in the front row, second from the right

The danger of the dance

The danger of the dance ...
Hot hands of strange boys
And bold eyes gone a little crazy
At the weekend ...
Dancing the waltz
And waiting to take you
Into a dark alley ...

Escaping with my coat,
I walk into the night alone,
my feet in burning shoes,
on snow and grit and ice.
Keep walking on ...
and underneath my coat,
my childish cardigan,
a comforting reminder
of my age,
or lack of it,
covers my temptress dress
and takes me home,
through the quiet snow
and an owl
outside my bedroom window.

50/50

It was always a struggle to persuade my mother to let me go to 50/50, the local Saturday night dance at the King's Hall. Girls at school were going, I told her ... my friend Jackie was going and other older girls. This seemed to be exactly the reason why I shouldn't go, in her mind. But, as I had spent the afternoon running up a skirt from a yard of fabric from the remnant shop, she had to relent, on the proviso that my brother kept an eye on me there.

You go in the door and pay, then give your coat to Mrs Birkenshaw in the ladies cloakroom and she gives you a ticket. You can hear the band already and smell the perfume and the cigarette smoke. It's already a long way from school. I look in the big mirror and wish my cheeks weren't so pink. Some girls are frothing up their underskirts, hitching up their stockings and spraying large amounts of lacquer on precipitous beehive hairdos.

The ornate dance hall is divided into two sections. In one pillared ballroom is sedate Old Tyme dancing where straight-backed shiny-haired men in white gloves and black suits, high stiff white collars, bow ties and patent leather shoes hold plump rosy-cheeked smiling ladies, elbows high,

Dangerous nights at the 50/50

chins up, in whirlwinds of pastel net, or clouds of chiffon, stepping out in sparkly shoes, twirling and scooping and sliding across a viciously polished wooden floor. It is a world that has never changed for them, in their lifetime.

Bradley Hustwick and his band proudly play the music they have always played, heads up, smartly executing the military two-step, the drummer faithfully accentuating the down beat and with little drum rolls to help it all along.

Meanwhile, in the adjacent hall is a seething mass of young people dancing to swing and quickstep music, performed by Eddie Bell and the Bell Boys in maroon tuxedos on the dusty velvet-curtained stage. Red fire buckets full of sand and cigarette ends are hanging, ready for any eventuality, on either side. The band is struggling with "Carolina Moon".

"We're a saxophone light," Bernard had said when they were coming on the bus tonight from Burley. "Colin's let us down again."

"You can't rely on that bloke, Bernard," Ray said, "I'd rather not have two saxophones at all, if 'e's going to be that unreliable."

"Well, Ray," said Bernard, "We'll 'ave to manage with just the one tonight, that's all."

On the stage, the young handsome drummer has a coolly detached manner, flicking the drums with his brush as if he's swatting flies, smoking and winking at the occasional girl. Slouching boys with slicked back hair, some with pastel-coloured drape jackets and crepe-soled shoes, steer cool-skinned girls in pointed bras, with bouffant lacquered hairdos, bottom-hugging skirts and stilettos, round the polished floor to a slow quick-step. A suntanned soldier on leave, still in uniform, is dancing in a loving embrace with the girl he hasn't seen for six months.

In one corner by the band some girls are dancing with each other, a different dance. They are trying out some new rock 'n' roll steps, learnt from going to the Mecca in Leeds, and have a nonchalant confidence, hands hanging from limp wrists, eyes staring blankly into the distance, chewing gum. They dance together, not with a boy. Suddenly some boys come and break them up and steer them off, giggling, into the crowd and start to dance together, doing the new steps.

The caretaker, Jimmy Elder, stands in his green overalls by an ornate pillar, leaning on a large brush, watching this carousel of potential social wildfire drift past and wonders what this world is coming to.

After a while, there is an ominous drum roll and the band stops playing and takes a break. This is the moment everyone has been waiting for; the moment when the latest records, bought each week from the electricians round the corner, are played. Antiquated speakers blast as the amplifier squeals into action, deafening everybody. The music starts.

Little Richard tears through the pillared hall and sends the place wild, splitting the air with "Rip It Up".

"Well it's Saturday night an' I just got paid, fool about my money, don't try to save. My heart says go go, have a time, cos it's Saturday night and I feel fine, gonna rip it up."

A sudden seething frenzy as dancers whirl and jump into action, some doing steps only just learnt, practised at work or at home in the kitchen holding onto the sink, or at school in break time. Now it's time to perform and the girls are twirling, paper-nylon underskirts crackling and layers of net frothing over long skinny legs, or short fat girls with pink faces showing stocking tops and bra straps, arms flailing, faces set in deep concentration. Boys, some with cigarettes dangling from mouths, with broad, padded shoulders, leaning determinedly, hot hands holding, letting go and holding again, the wild powdery faced black-eyed pink lipped twirly girls.

The music plays on and after a while, some of the girls retreat into the ladies cloakroom to fix their kiss-curls and rebellious blonde beehives, to adjust underskirts and re-apply scent and make-up while confiding in each other and giggling behind their hands, looking at one another, wide-eyed in the big mirror.

"What? No! The one in the blue jacket?"

And more giggling, more whispering, pink mouths open in disbelief.

"Ee didn't!"

"Ee did an' all!" says Julie from the telephone exchange who hears everything. She smiles wickedly, sniffs nonchalantly and pats her hair, looking closely in the mirror at a spot on her nose.

Sharply pointed bras, having been somewhat flattened by close dancing, are restored to their usual shape and waspie belts are readjusted. A cloud of hair lacquer, hitting the girl behind in the eye, now gives the finishing touch to the sculpted french pleat on busty blonde Maureen's beehive.

"I'm off back inter t'dance now," she announces dully to no one, sniffing and throwing her cigarette end into a fire bucket.

"Tarrah love!" says Mrs Birkenshaw, the cloakroom attendant, lighting another cigarette and looking at her watch.

Back in the dance hall Elvis is singing "Let's have a party!" and the shy girl from the post office suddenly drops all inhibitions, having found a kindred spirit in the butcher's dangerous looking delivery boy and is now learning how to do french kissing behind one of the pillars.

The posh, lanky public schoolboy from across the river, having mistakenly walked into the wrong dance on the wrong week, is doing the Charleston, the only dance he knows, quite suggestively with fat Janice from Burley, his eyes transfixed by her push-up bosoms and her irresistible squint.

A fixed grin on his face, he suddenly misses his footing and plummets backwards into the stomach of the local hoodlum. Before he can stammer an apology he gets a hard punch on the nose.

"Oh, I say! That bloody well hurts!" he says through a stream of blood. Then, remembering his school boxing training, he gathers his fists and floors the other boy with one swift blow. Girls scream. The boy on the floor gets up slowly and, face purple with rage, rams a large fist into the posh boy who staggers backwards, hitting his head on the ornate pillar and dropping gracefully to the floor, smiling but unconscious, blood now streaming from his nose and his ear.

The music stops. Jimmy Elder, who has seen a few injured revellers in his lifetime, now takes command. "Right! Somebody got a car? Got to get this lad into 'ospital, right sharp!"

The butcher's lad, disentangling himself from the arms of the no-longer-shy post office girl, runs over and, gently and effortlessly, picks up the unconscious boy. He's used to carrying sides of beef around at the slaughterhouse on Mondays.

"I'll tek 'im in me van now," he says to Jimmy calmly. Then, turning and looking straight at the thug, he narrows his eyes and says, "An' I'll see you later!" and walks off, carrying the boy in his arms across the polished floor, through the crowd, leaving a trail of blood behind.

The maroon tuxedos now return to the stage, adjust the microphone and launch into "In the Mood".

Grandpa's last trial

My grandfather, William Bradley, was a great man. At the age of twenty he was working as a civil engineer in Canada on the prairie, involved in the construction of bridges on the Canadian Pacific Railroad. He roughed it with the other workers, some of them dangerous knife-wielding fugitives, sleeping in flea-ridden huts and in winter washing with snow.

When he wasn't working he stayed on his uncle's farm on the prairie and rode a brown and white pinto pony bareback. When I was small he showed me the scars on his hands from when he had tried in vain to free it from a barbed wire fence. Sometimes at the farm they were visited by the Indian chief and members of his tribe. He sat motionless on his horse, waiting for Uncle Will to go out. He fetched a side of beef and slung it over the back of one of their horses. Then the chief made a signal and a sack of corn was produced and thrown to the ground. The chief raised his hand and they rode off. When they had gone, my grandfather asked his uncle why he'd given them so much. "They'll burn my farm down if I don't!" he said.

*William Bradley winning the hill climb on
"Felix", his unstoppable Bradley-Scott motorbike*

There was a beautiful girl back in Addingham and, while home on leave, my grandfather decided to marry her. She didn't want to leave the village so he stayed and built a workshop. The car was the great new invention and people needed repairs, parts and petrol. If he hadn't got the part he made a die and cast it. An inventor and a genius, his reputation grew and his motto was, "Nothing is impossible!" He built a motorbike out of some Scott parts, swopped with his friend, Mr Scott himself, in exchange for a typewriter. He worked day and night to perfect it in his draughty corrugated iron-roofed workshop.

He named the bike Felix after the cartoon cat because, like Felix in the popular song at the time, he "kept on walking". Felix was, in its day, unstoppable. With a front-wheel drive, six speeds and a water-cooled engine, it won trophies for hill climbing all over the north of England. My grandfather said that if it had the adhesion it could climb a vertical wall. In trials he would ride on the tops of walls and up near-vertical slopes to win. Some competitors would just scratch from the list if they saw that Bill Bradley had entered, knowing they hadn't a chance in hell of beating him.

One day in 1960, when he was in his seventies, he asked me to ride sidecar with him on a veterans' trial which was going to take us across the moors over a trial route he knew from days of old. He came to collect me, drawing up astride Felix, its loud roar filling our quiet road. He sat in overalls and cap as I climbed into the bullet-nosed silver sidecar. "There's a few bottles of water and some oil in there," he chuckled, "which we might need to use on the way!"

With a wave to my slightly anxious mother and hysterical dog, we set off. The problem with front-wheel drive bikes is that they don't turn sharply and have to take bends gently. The journey was loud but sedate, rather like a royal procession, its approach being advertised well in advance by its noise. People were not quite sure what to expect and stood, mouths open, staring at the empty street corner, then jumped slightly when the source of the noise came into view.

We assembled on the car park in the centre of Ilkley among many other veterans and their assorted motorbikes. There was a great atmosphere of camaraderie as they greeted old pals and chuckled about old times, wandering round each other's bikes, kicking wheels and testing brakes.

"Yer not expectin' ter get far on that, are yer?"

"I 'ope yer've brought yer tow rope!"

"By 'eck, that'll teck some watter!"

Caps and helmets were rammed firmly on heads, gloves pulled on, goggles and scarves arranged and engines were revved amid loud bangs and tooting of horns.

Grandpa basked in the limelight and always drew the attention of the press and public with the famous Felix. He fired up his engine, nearly deafening nearby spectators who scattered in all directions, leaving him chuckling and lighting up his pipe.

Once again I climbed into the long pointed silver sidecar with "Felix" written in a large confident scrawl. Grandpa revved up and, to cheers from the crowd, we were off in a cloud of smoke and a few bangs, roaring across the car park and turning down Brook Street.

Soon we were scrambling high over a rough moorland track flanked by heather and bracken, ditches on either side, Felix's throaty roar already beginning to deafen me in my right ear. High up beside me, pipe held between his teeth, Grandpa sailed through the blue sky, his big gnarled hands holding onto the handlebars as if it was the wild pinto pony on the prairie. We turned down through a narrow rocky track, flanked by a dry stone wall. Sheep fled, woolly tails whirling like propellers, pale grey eyes turned to the heavens, as this roaring monster ploughed its way

Grandpa with my mother, Rosa, (sitting in the sidecar on Bert, his usual passenger) on a hill climb victory ride at Clifton Hill

William Bradley, aged 85, standing proudly in front of a picture of him conquering Hepolite Scar on Felix, his two-wheel drive Bradley-Scott. It was the first motorbike and sidecar outfit ever to do so. The bike was called Felix? with a big question mark beside it, because there was a cartoon character cat called Felix and, in the song at the time, "Felix kept on walking", whatever happened. Grandpa's bike was unstoppable!

through them and up a steep bank onto a hilltop. After a while and with much hopping in and out on my part to push when we became a little stuck, or jumping up and down in the sidecar to "give it more purchase", it became clear that we were running out of petrol. It also became clear that we were a little off course, as there was a worrying lack of other competitors around and it was getting late.

We found ourselves on the top of a hill with a gentle track leading down to a stream. From this hill we could see the comforting and civilised scene of a family having a picnic, a checked tablecloth with sandwiches and cups of tea beside the stream, their sleek, pale blue Jaguar parked nearby. Grandpa stood, hands on hips, looking down at them. He removed his cap and shouted "Cooeeh!" as if he was calling in cows. This was a sound that the family would have preferred to ignore. What is more, they seemed reluctant to admit it could have anything possibly to do with them as they suddenly gazed in the opposite direction, pretending to have seen an invisible skylark. But another more persistent call, accompanied by a whistle - the sort my mother said went right through her - did the trick and their collective heads twizzled round and gazed up towards us. They seemed quite unaware of the important role they were about to play.

"Hello, I've got a bit of a problem!" Grandpa said with a little laugh. "We seem to have run out of gas!" The man opened his small mouth, shut it again and squinted back at us, as if a little deaf. Then, realising he had no choice, he beckoned us down. Before any obstacle could be presented, Grandpa produced from nowhere a length of rubber tubing and proceeded to siphon petrol from the tank of the gleaming Jag. He then spat loudly and filled a can with petrol. We offered to pay but they seemed happy to just wave us goodbye.

Off we roared, up a steep bank and onto a moorland road. It was getting late. Some riders were returning. "Where were yer, Bill?" and other words of comfort were yelled as they roared past. So we set off back, over the narrow unlit moorland road with deep ditches on either side. It was now that Grandpa announced, "D'yer know, love? These lights aren't working properly."

A faint beam squeezed from the large front light but not enough to light our way safely home, three miles along a darkening road. It was time to employ a little technology. "Keep an eye out for the ditch on your side, love," said Grandpa, and he started to trumpet a familiar little tune, one I had heard throughout my life with him. It was a tune of victory and fearless endeavour and rose up into the night air as we rode along, large moths flying into the faded beam, sheep staring at us with mad glowing eyes. "We'll get there in the end!" he said with a little laugh that was more like a cough.

Suddenly, there were bright beams of light behind us and loud roaring engines. A voice yelled, "Yer alright, Willie?" I looked over my shoulder and saw coming up behind us three leather-clad lads on powerful motorbikes. They drew alongside us, waving.

"Hey! By 'eck!" Grandpa shouted over the din. "What are you doing here?"

"We've come ter see yer 'ome, Willie, yer'll be alreet now!" they yelled, revving their bikes.

I was sitting looking at them with a certain amount of fear, visualising us lying beaten up in a ditch. They saw my concern. "It's OK loove, we're from Addingham! We know 'im!" they chorused, laughing. "We knew summat was wrong so we came lookin' for 'im, known 'im since we were little lads! We 'ang about 'is garige! Ee mends our bikes!" another one piped up.

Our road lit by the strong beams of this rowdy motorcade, we were escorted across the moor and back down into the valley and the lights of Ilkley. We thanked them and stood and waved as they roared off into the night waving and shouting, "Tarrah Willie!" and we went home for a cup of tea.

When I was little, I often went to stay at Grandpa's in Addingham at the weekend. As I wandered about his workshop he showed me how things worked. The lathes looked like elephants with trunks, metal worms came off the machines and went into milky liquid. Chains lifted heavy weights just by using your finger and all sorts of other miracles happened.

At night I always slept in Grandpa's big bed with a bolster down the middle and held his big hand which smelled of carbolic soap as I drifted off to sleep. He slept in a long sleeved vest and long johns and his hands smelled of oil, coal tar soap and tobacco. I slept with his hand under my head or holding his hand to my nose.

Bedtime stories were never boring, of fighting a knife-wielding crazy man in the cabin, standing him on his head and making him say, "Quits!" There were tales of riding his pinto pony across the prairie and of lying on his back in the creek shooting turkeys for his aunt. She would wake him up early in the morning shouting, "Will! There's turkeys in the creek! Be sharp! Go out and get me one for dinner!"

He told me stories of papering the walls in his uncle's farm on the prairie with copies of the Toronto Herald because his aunt said she wanted something to read. He told me of washing in snow each morning when he was on the gang, building the Canadian Pacific Railroad.

Before he went to sleep each night, he unravelled a crepe bandage from his leg and wound it into a ball. He had broken his leg many years ago when it got caught between his motorbike and the running board of a passing car, on the road from Addingham to Ilkley. His leg was so badly smashed that the doctor wanted to amputate it but Grandpa wouldn't let him and said he could fix it by bandaging it. He did this every day and saved the leg. Every morning I went to the foot of the bed and he threw the bandage towards me like a streamer, I caught it and he rewound it, with me hanging on to the other end, crawling up the bed until it was in a perfect ball. This was our game every morning. Then he bandaged his leg, round and round from knee to ankle, finished with a safety pin.

Grandpa was a great inspiration to me, encouraging me to use my imagination at every stage of my life. When I came to London in 1963 he sent me the very newest little transistor radio for my birthday so I could have music and news wherever I went. He came down to see me later on in the 1960s, getting on buses and shaking hands with the driver and the conductor and thanking them when we got off, much to their amazement.

"I want to see your life, how you live," he said and walked down the Kings Road with me, chatting to shopkeepers and ending up at the Chelsea Antique Market at the now famous Michael Costiff and Gerlinde's café upstairs where everyone who was creative used to meet in those days. Within ten minutes he was holding court at a big table surrounded by the regular customers, now famous but in those days just starting out, including Duggie Fields and Manolo Blahnik. They would sit open mouthed as this old man talked of climbing steep hills on his motor bike, of his adventures among the "Red Indians", of life on his uncle's farm on the prairie in Canada and even of the planets and other scientific things. He had an enthralled audience. One came over to me and said, "He's amazing, your Grandpa! He knows about ... just ... well, everything!"

He died at the age of 98, still bright in mind, in hospital with a bad chest infection. He smoked a pipe or cigarettes, up till the last!

Christmas Eve in Ilkley 1969

O n Christmas Eve I finally arrived, after five hours on a freezing smoke-filled train from London, the last train from Leeds into Ilkley station. Snow lay in the streets and tipsy or just plain drunk revellers squealed and shouted as they slid about on the icy pavements under the twinkling trees.

Clad in mini skirt, fur coat, knee high suede boots and clutching the usual overweight suitcase, I found a taxi. The driver seemed relieved.

"Very busy tonight, Miss, lots of crazy people about," he said, shaking his head and nodding at the same time. He was from India, I discovered, and drove me through the glittering streets, dropping me by the snow-laden privet hedge outside our house. Bidding him a happy Christmas, he shaking his head in reply, I teetered down the silent icy path and climbed the back steps.

The kitchen door immediately flew open and the dog hurled itself into the night and did a lap round the garden while my mother hugged me and looked at me, holding my face in her hands, smiling.

"Oh love! Look at your eyelashes! Have you been smoking? I can smell it!" and we sat down and had a cup of tea. My father was down at the church, preparing for the ritual carol playing on the bells at midnight. This was done every Christmas Eve by members of the family, brothers and sisters of my father, in the freezing cold bell tower. They stood next to each bell and held the clapper in fur gloved hands, beating out each note of the carols in perfect synchronicity. To reach the bell tower meant an almost vertical climb up steep stone steps.

"Oh, can I go?! I said foolishly and went sliding and slipping down the road to the church. To get to the bell tower, I had to climb on all fours up the dark steps which were worn smooth by years of use. I suddenly realised this was a bad dream, my breath coming out in white clouds but it was too late to turn back. Round and round I climbed, the narrow unforgiving spiral that my fifteen-stone father had run up and down like a mountain goat, four times every Sunday of his life.

Finally I reached the bell chamber. There stood the group of eight, muffled to the eyebrows in fur coats, heavy gloves and rugby scarves, loudly greeting me, each member of the family standing by their individual bell, ready to begin. I hoisted myself into the ancient, deep stone window sill and sat, knees up to chin, waiting for the show to begin. A softly spoken command ... a nod ... and then the first great bell was struck by Auntie Edna with leopard fur-gloved hand. The first minor note of "Silent Night" rang out across the valley. This was greeted in the streets below by the loud cheers of the revellers, surprised and enchanted by what they were hearing.

*Diana's father, Mac Crawshaw, the chief bell-ringer at Ilkley
Parish Church, with a young Alan Titchmarsh,
whom he taught to ring, standing behind him*

Each bell-ringer struck their bell carefully, with whispered commands, giggles and reprimands as they played in almost perfect synchronicity.

Then the slow careful notes of "The First Noel" wafted through the night. Large, white snowflakes fluttered through the darkness of the sky behind me, like bits of cotton wool, lit by the moon.

Later, bell-ringing done, we all walked down to "Glenhome", the place where the family was born and raised and, after a brief but very loud rendering of "Ding Dong Merrily on High" the door was flung open and we were welcomed into a warm kitchen smelling of giblets and cigars and hugged and kissed by the rest of the family.

Diana has lived and worked in London since the 1960s as a fashion designer for such companies as Dollyrocker, Mr Freedom, Secret Ingredient and many other King's Road shops. In the 1990s life changed. With the encouragement of Richard Branson, who invited her to "read a few hands" of his staff in his Virgin office and then the cargo division at Heathrow, competing with the roar of low flying aircraft, she became a full time palmist and tarot reader at Wilde Ones, a crystal shop in the King's Road.

She grows grapes, apples, vegetables and old roses on her allotment, listening to birds and Radio 3, watched by frogs in three very murky ponds.